T0288715

Ladders

NORTH ATLANTIC COAST

WHERE ON EARTH?

Read to find out about the geography of the North Atlantic coast.

Rugged Coast

by Brett Gover

Lighthouses help boaters navigate the North Atlantic coast. This lighthouse is in Maine.

A seagull flies along the North Atlantic coast. It travels from Maine to Virginia. What does it see as it moves south?

In the north, the gull flies over Maine. The rocky coastline twists and turns where the ocean meets the land. This forms large bodies of water called **bays** and smaller bodies of water called **coves**. The gull sees fishing villages, harbors, and small islands along the coast.

Farther south, the coastline becomes straighter and less rocky. Larger towns and cities appear. The gull goes by New Hampshire and then Massachusetts. It passes Boston and the famous outline of Cape Cod. A **cape** is a point of land that sticks out into the ocean.

South of Rhode Island and Connecticut, the land pokes out into the ocean even more. Below are the tall buildings of New York City. Then the gull flies over New Jersey, Delaware, and Maryland. Soon, it is soaring over beach towns, pine forests, and long, narrow islands.

After crossing the mouth of Chesapeake (CHESS-uh-peek) Bay, the gull reaches Virginia. The land along the coast is now flat, not hilly. The gull has traveled about 800 miles along a rugged coast.

Where on Earth?

THE NORTH ATLANTIC COAST

There are many cool things to know about the North Atlantic coast. Many kinds of animals live there. People built some of the oldest and most important cities in the United States there. Here are some fun facts about the North Atlantic states.

Maine

Vermont

New Hampshire

New York

Massachusetts

Rhode Island

Connecticut

Pennsylvania

New Jersey

Delaware

Maryland

Virginia

New Hampshire

Many large whales swim past the North Atlantic coast. Places such as New Hampshire run whale watching tours. People can see humpback whales such as this one up close.

New Jersey

Different weather systems meet near the North Atlantic coast. Sometimes they mix to make surprise superstorms. In 2012, Superstorm Sandy hit the coast of New Jersey. It caused billions of dollars in damage.

Maine

In 2012, a lobster weighing 27 pounds was caught off the coast of Maine. The 40-inch-long beast was returned to the ocean.

Moose Peak Lighthouse on Mistake Island in northern Maine is the foggiest place on the Atlantic coast.

Massachusetts

Harvard University (above) is the oldest college in the United States.

Boston, Massachusetts, is a city of first things. People built the first lighthouse, first public park, and first subway in the United States there. They set up the first public school and first college there. It was also the first U.S. city to host a marathon race each year.

Rhode Island

Rhode Island is the smallest U.S. state. You could put Rhode Island into Alaska, the largest state, about 425 times.

New York

The area from Boston to Washington, D.C., is a **megalopolis**, a large area of closely connected cities. It covers more than 400 miles and holds more than one-sixth of the people living in the United States. It includes Philadelphia and Baltimore. It also includes New York City (above), the nation's largest city, which is in the state of New York. The Statue of Liberty stands in New York Harbor.

Check In How does the coastline change throughout the North Atlantic region?

5

Pools of WOND

by Brett Gover

> These children explore tide pools at Odiorne Point State Park in New Hampshire.

Whoosh! Water crashes on

the coast of Maine. Creatures that live here feel this rhythm of the **tides** every day.

Tides are all about gravity. The gravity of the sun pulls on Earth. The moon's gravity pulls, too. As Earth spins, gravity pulls ocean water over some shores. It pulls water away from other shores. This causes the tides. During "high tide" on the coast of Maine the ocean covers most of the beach. About six hours later, more of the beach is uncovered. It is "low tide." The water stays farther out in the sea.

Animals near the shore live in homes that change during the day. During high tide, their homes are covered by the ocean. When the tide goes out, their homes are uncovered. Pools of seawater called **tide pools** are left behind between the rocks.

Life can be hard for the creatures in tide pools. High tide sometimes carries large, hungry fish into tide pools. At low tide, the hot sun shines on tide pool creatures. Hungry birds and other animals can easily catch and eat them. What will you find in a tide pool? Let's take a look.

Be an Explorer

When is the best time to explore tide pools? Go during low tide or after a big storm. That's when the water level is lowest. Here are some of the creatures you might discover.

CLAMS are animals with soft bodies. Their two round shells are stuck together on one side so they can open and close. A clam closes its shell to stay safe from danger.

MUSSELS are like clams. However, their shells are usually darker and not as round.

SEA ANEMONES (uh-NEHM-uh-neez) look like beautiful plants, but they are animals. They have long **tentacles**, or armlike structures. Their tentacles can sting animals with poison. Then anemones eat their catch.

CRABS are hard-shelled creatures. They walk sideways on ten legs. Watch out for their pinching claws!

PERIWINKLES are snails. They eat tiny plantlike creatures called **algae** (AL-jee). Algae can grow on tide pool rocks. Birds that live near the shore like to eat periwinkles.

SEA URCHINS live at the bottom of tide pools. They are covered with long, sharp, poisonous spines.

Ready, Set, Explore!

Exploring a tide pool can be dangerous. Always make sure an adult is around and follow these tips.

DO:

Walk carefully. Wet, algae-covered rocks can be slippery.

Research the tide schedule for the day so you can plan for the best time to see the pools.

Ask questions. There are many different kinds of creatures in tide pools. Be curious and talk about what you see.

Touch animals gently. Don't pry animals off rocks. Return anything you do move to the spot where you found it.

Take notes. Describe the animals you see. Take pictures or draw the creatures so that you'll remember them later.

DON'T:

Walk in tide pools. You can disturb or harm animals if you walk in tide pools. You could also hurt yourself on an animal's poisonous stinger or sharp spine.

Lose sight of the ocean. Big waves can catch you by surprise.

Take anything home. Starfish are pretty, but if you take one out of its pool, it will die. Leave the starfish in their homes when you go back to yours.

SEA STARS, or starfish, have hard, spiny skin. Most sea stars have five arms, but some have more. They use those arms to pry open the shells of clams and mussels.

RED ALGAE usually grow in salt water. Most red algae spend their lives attached to rocks. Algae provide oxygen to tide pools.

Check In What are some of the rules for safely checking out tide pools? Why are these rules important?

Read to find out about the kinds of jobs people do on the North Atlantic coast.

Boats, Bogs, and Bolts

by Brett Gover

> Tourists float on Swan Boats in Boston's Public Garden. The boats have been a popular attraction since 1877.

For thousands of years, people have lived and worked along the North Atlantic Ocean.

First, Native Americans found what they needed to live here. They grew their food. They hunted animals from the land and fished in the sea. Then in the 1600s, settlers from Europe began to arrive. They built fishing and farming villages along the coast.

Some of these villages grew into towns and cities. In less than 100 years, cities such as Baltimore and Boston grew. Fishing and farming also grew. Businesses built factories that needed workers. Many people moved from small towns to larger communities to work in these factories.

Early factories made goods such as metal tools and **textiles**, or cloth. Later, factories made automobiles, submarines, plastics, and chemicals. The Atlantic coastline was full of natural harbors. This made it a good place for shipping, or transporting goods by water. Huge ships carried products to other places.

Today, tourism is another important industry there. Millions of visitors come to see the busy cities. Tourists also enjoy beaches, boating trips, historical sites, and the beautiful coast.

Crabbing IN THE CHESAPEAKE BAY

At a seafood market in Norfolk, Virginia, many customers shop for blue crabs. Less than 12 hours ago, these shellfish were in Chesapeake Bay. How did they get to the market so quickly?

Joe the crab fisherman could show you. Every morning, Joe and his crew rise before dawn. They load their boat with the tools they need to go crabbing. They pack long poles with hooks on one end. They pack wooden baskets, rubber gloves, and bait.

Out on the bay, they stop at a line of colorful **buoys**. A chain connects each buoy to a large wire trap called a crab pot. The pot sits at the bottom of the bay. Joe's crew has put bait in each pot. Crabs crawl into the pots to eat this bait. The crabs are now trapped. At each buoy, the crew uses the hooked pole to pull up the pot by its chain. Then they dump crabs onto a sorting table. The crew wears gloves. Otherwise they might get pinched!

After putting new bait in each pot, Joe drops the pot back into the water. He checks several lines of buoys. By mid-afternoon, Joe and his crew have checked all of their 250 crab pots. Joe returns to Norfolk to sell the crabs to the buyers waiting there.

> Maryland blue crabs come from Chesapeake Bay. They get their name from the male crab's blue pinchers. The female blue crab has red pinchers. Both males and females are prized for their tasty meat.

A crab fisherman pulls a crab trap out of the water off the coast of Virginia Beach, Virginia.

Cranberry Farming IN MASSACHUSETTS

Think of a farm. Do you picture rows of crops in a field? You probably don't picture a **bog**, or wet, spongy ground. However, one of the North Atlantic coast's top crops comes from bogs: cranberries!

Cranberries grow on vines with roots in a bog's spongy soil. At first the berries are green and tiny. Soon they grow larger. In the fall, the berries turn colors like leaves do. When they're bright red, they're ready for picking.

In southeastern Massachusetts, Belinda runs a cranberry farm. It has been in her family for more than 75 years. In the past, the work was done mainly by hand. Today, it is done mostly by machine.

Belinda uses wet harvesting to pick most of her berries. Workers fill the bog with water. Then they drive through it in big-wheeled vehicles. That makes the berries shake loose from their vines and float to the top of the water. There, the workers use boards to push the berries onto a conveyor belt. The belt dumps them into a truck, which carries them to a factory. There, workers turn them into cranberry sauce, dried cranberries, or cranberry juice.

> Workers gather cranberries floating in a flooded bog in Massachusetts.

The corralled cranberries are lifted by conveyer belt and then loaded into a truck. This worker is smoothing the piles on this almost full truck. Next stop for these cranberries will be the processing plant.

Shipyard Welding IN MAINE

Raul is not short. However, at work he often feels tiny. He helps build and fix large ships. Some ships are as long as two football fields. Raul is a welder at a shipyard in Maine.

Welding is a way of joining pieces of metal. A welder uses a tool called a welding torch. The welding torch makes high heat that melts metal. Two soft pieces of metal grow cool and hard. Then they are stuck together. Raul is usually welding together the pieces of metal that form a ship's sides and bottom.

Welding is dangerous work. It makes hot sparks and loud noises that can hurt a worker. Heavy boots and leather gloves protect Raul's feet and hands. He wears special clothing that will not catch fire. Safety glasses and a helmet protect his eyes and face. Earplugs block much of the noise.

People have built ships in Maine for more than 400 years! In the past, shipbuilders chose to work near the coast. Many kinds of wood grew in the thick forests. The shipbuilders used the wood to make different ship parts. Today, the ships are mostly made of metal.

Building a ship can take years. When each ship is ready, Raul is proud of his work.

The USS *Sir Winston Churchill* is a U.S. Navy ship built at the Bath Iron Works in Bath, Maine.

A welder uses his torch to repair the hull of a ship.

Check In Choose one of the jobs you read about and explain how that worker earns a living on the coast.

Lighting Up the Coastline

by David Holford

A ship is traveling from Nova Scotia, Canada, to New York. Strong winds and heavy rain make it hard to see. The scared crew doesn't know where to go. Suddenly a light shines ahead. It shows that there are rocks near the shore. Now the ship can move safely around the rocks.

Lighthouses do an important job. They shine a strong beam of light to warn **navigators**, or the crew members who tell a ship where to go. The light means there are dangers nearby, such as rocks or shallow seas. Lighthouses also help navigators figure out where they are if they get lost in fog or a storm.

There are more than 120 lighthouses along the North Atlantic coastline. Most are open to visitors. Lighthouses come in many shapes and sizes. People visit them to learn about their history and see how they work.

∧ Marshall Point Lighthouse near Port Clyde, Maine, was built in 1832. Today, more than 60 lighthouses line Maine's rocky coast.

Built to Last

In the early 1700s, people built the first lighthouses in the United States on the North Atlantic coast. Some were made of wood. Most were round towers made of bricks or stone. Later, people used steel and concrete. With such strong materials, people could build lighthouses that were tough enough to stand in the water. They could also build lighthouses that were differently shaped. However, the tall, round tower is still the most common type.

Early lighthouses like this one in Newport, Rhode Island, were often made of wood. They might be part of a house, such as a lighthouse keeper's home. Not many wooden lighthouses are left today.

Skeletal lighthouses can be made of thin strips of metal. They use fewer materials and are very light. This design is often used for lighthouses built on sand or mud so that they won't sink. Stairs run inside a column in the middle. This lighthouse is in Marblehead, Massachusetts.

Stone lighthouses are made of concrete, brick, and other rock. They have thick bottoms to hold up the weight of all the stone. This is Old Cape Henry Lighthouse, and it is a historic landmark. It sits near the black-and-white lighthouse (at left) that is used today.

Cast-iron lighthouses are easier and cheaper to build than brick and stone lighthouses. They also don't need to be fixed often. Cape Henry Lighthouse in Virginia (shown here) is one of the tallest cast-iron lighthouses in the United States.

What's Inside?

Today, most lighthouses are **automated**. Machines do the work for people. For example, a lighthouse keeper's main job used to be to light the lamp with a bright fire every night. Today, an electric light comes on every night automatically in most lighthouses. Modern features are built into new lighthouses and added to historic ones. Read about some of the working parts of the Cape Cod, Massachusetts, lighthouse shown on this page.

The lantern room is at the top of the tower. It holds the light, or "lamp." The lamp needs to shine its light over a large area. To do this, it has a motor that turns the lamp when it is lit. The light seems to move across the ocean. A catwalk or narrow walkway runs outside the lantern room. It lets people clean the lighthouse's windows.

In fog, the light cannot be seen far from shore. Then a foghorn on top of the lighthouse blows every few seconds to warn ships. On some lighthouses, antennas send out warning signals to ship radios during fog and storms.

Special lenses on the lamp make its light bigger and brighter. They also focus the light into a beam that can shine for more than 20 miles out to sea.

The lantern room is built on top of a tower. This raises the lamp high. Then its beam can be seen from miles out at sea. The strong tower can stand up to storms and wind.

The round lantern room at the top of the tower has windows on each side. The light can shine in all directions. The keeper can also see the coast and any ships passing by.

Only a spiral staircase will fit inside a lighthouse tower!

Race Point Lighthouse, Cape Cod, Massachusetts

Unique and Unusual

You've learned about lighthouses. You've seen how they have changed. Now check out these unique and unusual lighthouses. Some are even haunted!

Maine's West Quoddy Head Lighthouse is built at the farthest eastern point of the United States. Its picture is used on many calendars and travel posters.

Sheffield Island Lighthouse in Connecticut was built in 1868 and used for 34 years. Today it is a museum in the middle of a nature preserve.

The six-sided Drum Point Lighthouse used to stand in Maryland's coast. In 1975, people moved it from the water to the land outside a nearby museum.

Haunted Lighthouses

Cre-e-e-a-k . . . As you open the lighthouse door, something seems to push it back against you. After you enter, the door slams shut. You are alone, but it feels like someone else is there. Is this lighthouse haunted?

Some people think Point Lookout Lighthouse in Maryland is the most haunted lighthouse in the United States. Doors open and close for no reason. People hear voices, footsteps, and even snoring. However, no one is there. A prison camp for Civil War soldiers was once located nearby. Are prisoners haunting the lighthouse?

Is Maine's Owls Head Light haunted? Years ago the lighthouse keeper's three-year-old toddler woke her parents with a warning. She said, "Fog's rolling in! Time to put the foghorn on!" The warning came from her "imaginary friend." He looked like an old sea captain. Was he actually the ghost of a past keeper?

Check In   How do lighthouses protect ships on the North Atlantic coast?

25

WHERE WILD PONIES RUN

by Elizabeth Massie

> The wild ponies of Assateague come in many colors. These include brown, black, tan, and spotted brown and white.

A HERD OF WILD PONIES GALLOPS ALONG THE

sandy beach. The animals run freely across the land before stopping to eat grass. These are the wild ponies of Assateague (as-uh-TEEG) Island.

Assateague is a long, narrow **barrier island** off the coast of Maryland and Virginia. People do not remember a time when the ponies did not live here. They are only found in the southernmost part of the North Atlantic coast region. But where did these ponies come from? No one knows for sure. Some local legends say that a Spanish ship wrecked off the coast around the year 1600. People believe that these ponies are **descendants**, or relatives, of ponies that swam to the island's shore from the ship.

What's the difference between a horse and a pony? Ponies aren't young horses. They are smaller than other horses even when full grown.

On Assateague Island, the ponies live in a **refuge**. A refuge is a protected area where wildlife can run free. The ponies roam the beaches, dunes, and marshes of the refuge. There are no fences to stop them or stables to hold them. People do not live on the island. However, people do live on Chincoteague (shing-kuh-TEEG) Island nearby.

Tourists visit Assateague Island to hike, canoe and kayak, and camp. However, the main reason they come is to see the ponies. The ponies bring in many tourists. This helps businesses in surrounding communities.

Thousands of people from around the world come each year to watch the ponies swim the channel between Assateague and Chincoteague Islands.

When the weather gets cold the Assateague ponies grow thick winter fur that helps them stay warm.

THE PONY SWIM

Assateague Island only has space for some ponies to live. Each year since 1925, some ponies have been sold to make room. During the summer, a town on Chincoteague Island always has a "pony swim" and carnival.

Workers called saltwater cowboys help during this event. They move the ponies from the island into the **channel**, or narrow waterway, between Assateague and Chincoteague Islands. They wait for slack tide. Then the water in the channel is calm. That way the ponies can swim across safely. People watch the ponies parade through the carnival. The next day, after the young ponies are sold, the adult ponies swim back to the island.

The townspeople hold the sale each year because it helps both the town and the ponies. The sale helps to limit the number of ponies living on the island. The ponies that are sold get food and care. The money also pays for things the town needs.

KEEPING THE PONIES WILD

It's not a good idea for these ponies to have too much contact with people. Wild ponies act a different way if they are around people a lot. Some people in the community watch what happens when the ponies visit with tourists and people at the carnivals. They think being with people is making the ponies tamer, or less wild.

For example, the ponies are eating less of their normal foods. Many try to trick the tourists into giving them junk food. Adult ponies will gently push a baby pony in front of a slow car. When the car stops, the adult ponies come close to beg for food.

Junk food is not good for the ponies. Therefore, park rangers have made a rule to stop people from feeding the ponies. They tell people to stay at least ten feet away from the wild ponies. If the ponies can't get food from people, it might help them stay wild.

These ponies have just crossed the channel to Chincoteague Island. The pony sale keeps the herd living on the island to about 160 ponies.

Many kinds of grasses grow on Assateague Island. The ponies eat grass, along with plants such as rosehips and bayberry twigs.

Check In How do the ponies of Assateague affect the lives of the people living on Chincoteague?

Discuss

1. What connections can you make among the five selections that you read in this book? How are the selections related?

2. Choose a feature of the North Atlantic coast that is most interesting to you or that you'd like to learn more about. Explain your choice.

3. What is one danger that tide pool creatures face at high tide? What is one danger they face at low tide?

4. Of the three jobs described in the selection "Boats, Bogs, and Bolts," which one would you least like to do? Explain your choice.

5. How could the popularity of the ponies on Assateague Island help or hurt them?